A MANY-COLORED COAT OF DREAMS: THE POETRY OF COUNTEE CULLEN

Broadside Critics Series Number 4.
James A. Emanuel, General Editor

ABOUT THE SERIES COVER

The cord represents literary creativity which has a strong tradition among African peoples. The tradition is found in the great store of oral history, in the contextual writing which forms designs seen on buildings, calabashes and other useful objects. It is implicit in many figurative designs and sculpture.

Several times in the history of the people, the cord has been severed abruptly—but continues again in a rich store of literary works represented here in the Broadside Critics Series.

—Cledie Taylor

A MANY-COLORED COAT OF DREAMS:

THE POETRY OF COUNTEE CULLEN

by

Houston A. Baker, Jr.

bp

BROADSIDE PRESS
12651 Old Mill Place   Detroit, Michigan 48238

First Printing
First Edition
Copyright © 1974 by Houston A. Baker, Jr.

No part of this book can be copied, reproduced, or used
in any way without written permission from
Broadside Press, 12651 Old Mill Place, Detroit, Michigan 48238

LCN: 73-91266

ISBN: 0-910296-36-7

Manufactured in the United States of America

TO THE MEMORY OF
ARNA BONTEMPS

Acknowledgments

Grateful acknowledgments made for permission to use quotations from the following books:

From *Color* by Countee Cullen
Copyright, 1925 by Harper & Row, Publishers, Inc.; renewed, 1953 by Ida M. Cullen

From *Copper Sun* by Countee Cullen
Copyright, 1927 by Harper & Row, Publishers, Inc.; renewed, 1955 by Ida M. Cullen

From *The Black Christ* by Countee Cullen
Copyright, 1929 by Harper & Row, Publishers, Inc.; renewed, 1957 by Ida M. Cullen

From *The Ballad of the Brown Girl* by Countee Cullen
Copyright, 1929 by Harper & Row, Publishers, Inc.; renewed, 1957 by Ida M. Cullen

From *The Medea* by Countee Cullen
Copyright, 1935 by Harper & Row, Publishers, Inc.; renewed, 1963 by Ida M. Cullen

From *On These I Stand* by Countee Cullen
Copyright, 1947 by Harper & Row, Publishers, Inc.

By permission of the publishers, Harper & Row.

Contents

A MANY-COLORED COAT OF DREAMS:
THE POETRY OF COUNTEE CULLEN

A Many-Colored Coat of Dreams:
The Poetry of Countee Cullen

In *Caroling Dusk, An Anthology of Verse by Negro Poets,* Countee Cullen—whom one critic[1] describes as a time-bound author raised to prominence by a white vogue —gives his date of birth as May 30, 1903.[2] In that year, W. E. B. DuBois's *The Souls of Black Folk* appeared and astonished some critics with its forthright, scholarly, and hauntingly lyrical portrayal of the Black American situation. Paul Laurence Dunbar, the first Black American poet of distinction, had become an invalid (he died three years later of tuberculosis). *The Colonel's Dream,* released in 1905, marked the virtual end of Charles Chesnutt's career as a novelist. Though Dunbar and Chesnutt were looked upon with favor by the following generation, it was Du-Bois's brilliant collection that created a wave which crested during the Harlem Renaissance of the 1920s.

There is scant equivocation in *The Souls of Black Folk,* and the critic who finds no bitterness or militancy in it is simply myopic. When one probes the work, however, one finds that it is not radically out of harmony with its age. Dunbar, Chesnutt, and DuBois all wanted to be acknowledged authors, and the artistic standards they set for themselves were not far from those of the American mainstream. Chesnutt writes somewhat sentimental romances, and his letters contain a number of adulatory references to popular white American authors. DuBois's impressionistic style and his quotations from Browning, Schiller, and Swinburne display his Western orientation. And Dunbar lamented to James Weldon Johnson: "You know, of course, that I didn't start as a dialect poet. I simply came to the conclusion that I could write it as well, if not better, than anybody else I knew of, and that by doing so I should gain a hearing. I gained the hearing, and now they don't want me to write anything but dialect."[3]

The three authors were victims of the dilemma that DuBois describes as a "double consciousness"—the black man's sense that he is both an American and something apart. When Frances E. W. Harper wrote in 1861 to the editor of a recently established periodical, "we [Black authors] must look to the future which, God willing, will be better than the present or the past, and delve into the heart of the world,"[4] she captured the salient aspects of the problem. The future can always be seen as promising when one is chained to a white-dominated present, and a glance into "the heart of the world" may produce a more acceptable theme than a thoroughgoing analysis of one's oppressive situation—particularly when such an examination is likely to impress upon a white reader his own moral culpability. Simply stated, the problem is that of the Black man in a white country, of the Black author writing for a white public; and many thousands have perished in the resulting flood of emotions. In its more advanced form, the problem that beset DuBois, Chesnutt, and Dunbar raises an important artistic and aesthetic question. What is the task of the Black American author and by what standards is he to be judged?

If this query is placed in an historical context, it is relatively easy to gaze back on turn-of-the-century America and see that the odds were stacked against the Black writer who decided that he would give an unflinching portrayal of Black America, that he would make no compromises, and that he—like William Lloyd Garrison—would be heard. There were simply too many Jim Crow laws and lynchings (and too few courageous publishers) for such honesty to exist. And Black creativity, which was to flower

14

in the 1920s, faced many of the same handicaps. The age that witnessed the deportation of Marcus Garvey, the heroic but unsuccessful efforts of James Weldon Johnson to secure the passage of an anti-lynching bill, and the arrest of Ossian Sweet was scarcely one of interracial harmony. Although the chronological span between the end of Dunbar's career and the publication of Countee Cullen's first volume of poetry, *Color* (1925), is almost infinitesimal, critics have seemed unable to bring these twenty years into perspective. Some make it appear that the Harlem Renaissance was a self-willed affair, springing forth from the Black American consciousness like Athena from the brow of Zeus. Such writers see the 1920s as what the philosopher R. G. Collingwood calls an age of brilliance, historical evidence being abundant, and the era's major thought being accessible to human reason. It is a mistake, however, to assume that the difficulties that confronted Sutton Griggs, Charles W. Chesnutt, and W. E. B. DuBois disappeared during the 1920s as more desirable options opened for Black authors.

When one breaks the shell of contemporaneity by viewing history as a series of intrinsically related events, the problems of turn-of-the-century Black authors do not seem far removed from those faced by today's artists. Cataclysmic social, epistemological, and aesthetic changes do not occur with each passing decade. Paul Dunbar's "thee's" and "thou's," Countee Cullen's "albeit's" and "listeth's," Gwendolyn Brooks's polysyllabics, and Imamu Baraka's tortured and allusive verses are all intelligible within a brief historical continuum. Cultural goals and descriptive vocabularies may alter, but a dilemma such as the Black American's seldom disappears in seven or eight decades.

This is not to say that art never undergoes a sudden face-lifting. William Wordsworth dealt neo-classicism a deathblow in the *Lyrical Ballads,* and T. S. Eliot made a generation aware that it had come of age (and was lost) in *The Waste Land.* But the explicit question for the Black American writer and critic—given a specific historical context (1903-1973)—is how much the strategies employed by Black authors from Paul Laurence Dunbar to Don L. Lee have contributed to the melioration of the Black American dilemma. If the alternatives available today are equally undesirable, it seems simplistic to assert that one artistic manner has been more revolutionary than another. It would be just as simplistic to assume that the efforts of contemporary Black artists alone will make the years ahead more agreeable.

To consider art an agency of societal change is to accept certain a priori assumptions. First, one must adopt a socially oriented critical approach, and second, one must take for granted the realistic mode as the *sine qua non* of artistic expression. In "Criteria of Negro Art," DuBois approves both:

> . . . all Art is propaganda and ever must be, despite the wailing of the purists. I stand in utter shamelessness and say that whatever art I have for writing has been used always for propaganda for gaining the right of black folk to love and enjoy. I do not care a damn for any art that is not used for propaganda. But I do care when propaganda is confined to one side while the other is stripped and silent.[5]

Like the writings of Bernard De Mandeville, Samuel Butler, and Jean Paul Sartre, Black art is here defined in social terms; it should conduce toward "the right . . . to love and enjoy" and must act as a counterthrust to opposing societal patterns. The negative propaganda on one side of the "veil" described by Du Bois should occasion a resistant form of proselytizing. Inherent in this point of view is the realistic mode, for art that provides merely vicarious escapism will not suffice. Real human inequities have to be exposed, and proper attitudes and values need to be molded. Art, therefore, is conceived as a social institution, akin to government, religion, and law.

Within this framework, Shelley's dictum that poets are the "unacknowledged legislators of the world" becomes a normative, rather than a descriptive, statement. The poet not only puts forward the standards that his readers are to follow, but also holds up for their admiration the struggles

16

and individuals of the racial past that have conformed to such standards. The aim of the artist is always social change of a specific kind: he is concerned to bring the people into harmony with the overall design that he—and those who have shared in the creation of his mandate—have conceived. Such a view approximates the nineteenth-century aesthetic statements of Charles Saint-Simon and Auguste Comte and the more recent writings of Christopher Caudwell. Even a cursory reading of Mao's writings on literature and art followed by a perusal of *The Quotable Karenga* demonstrates the affinity between the doctrines of a number of socialist thinkers and the injunctions of today's non-white artists and aestheticians.

Black American literature came of age during the 1930s and 1940s when proletarian art was in its heyday, and Richard Wright was one of the first Black American authors to achieve overwhelming national and international success. If one adds to this fact the growth of an educated Black reading public, it is not difficult to understand why many writers of the fifties and sixties looked upon Wright as a paradigm for Black literature and included the 1920s in the nonage of their tradition. Wright's early fiction was read approvingly by many white Americans and Europeans, and his themes and aims were often in harmony with a socialistic ideal: propagandistic, oriented toward change, and conceived in accordance with a specific social philosophy. Though the Black American reaction to *Uncle Tom's Children* and *Native Son* was not entirely favorable, the National Association for the Advancement of Colored People did award Wright the Spingarn Medal in 1940; and he could feel a great deal more assurance than, say, Claude McKay or Langston Hughes in beginning their careers that Black America was amenable to proletarian art.

This historical and aesthetic perspective is necessary if one is to understand the position that Countee Cullen, who was called by contemporaries the poet laureate of the Harlem Renaissance, occupies in the gallery of writers that is being contemplated by today's artists, critics, and academicians. The space assigned to Cullen seems describable as a dimly lit and seldom-visited chamber where genteel souls stare forth in benign solicitude. Darwin Turner, for example, calls him "the lost Ariel,"[6] and Nathan Huggins speaks of Cullen clinging "quite tenaciously to the genteel tradition."[7] Such phrases only indicate that Cullen did not march to the beat of the drummer who has "boomlay, boomlay, boomlayed" us into the 1970s. But critics are often embarrassed by the poet who is out of step with the age, as though someone had brought out a picture of a nonpartisan ancestor and shown it to their most committed colleagues. There follow tacit dismissals, vague apologies, and overweening defenses.

Of course, the disconcerted responses of Black critics faced with the life and work of Countee Cullen are predicated upon certain progressivistic assumptions; e.g., the poet does not "lead" to the point at which Black authors find themselves today. Behind these assumptions, however, lies an intention that one critic would call a corralling of the Black artist into doing certain tasks;[8] there extends, in other words, the vista of social realism detailed above. Cullen did not think of art in Saint-Simonian or Caudwellian terms; his guiding mode was not the realistic but the romantic, and he believed the poet was a man in tune with higher spiritual forms rather than a social tactician. The romantic mode implies a world charged with wonder and suspends the laws of probability—there is unlimited expectation. Though piety and devotion are operative, the prevailing motive is love. Cullen's canon reflects all of these characteristics and contains the distinction between a dark romanticism of frustrated love and infidelity and a bright one of harmony and enduring friendship. The mode, or preshaping impulse, of his work is in harmony with his overall conception of the poet as a man who dwells above mundane realities; for Cullen, the poet is the dream keeper, the "man . . . endowed with more lively sensibility, more enthusiasm and tenderness," the individual who is "certain of nothing but of the holiness of the Heart's affection and the truth of Imagination." These quotations from Wordsworth and Keats are descriptive; they capture in brief the

18

a priori mandates of the romantic poet. In *"Cor Cordium,"* "To John Keats, Poet. At Springtime," "For a Poet," "To an Unknown Poet," and "That Bright Chimeric Beast," Cullen defines the poet as a creator of immortal beauty, a man still in harmony with the mysterious and the ideal in an age "cold to the core, undeified," a person who wraps his dreams in "a silken cloth" and lays them away in "a box of gold." Such an author is far removed from the ideal social artist and can hardly be compared to many of today's Black artists, who compose as though our lived realities were contingent upon their next quatrain. What we have, then, is not a difference in degree but one in kind. To apply the standards of a socially oriented criticism to Countee Cullen and dismiss him is to achieve no more than a pyrrhic victory. To expect the majority of his work to consist of the type of idiomatic, foot-tapping, and right-on stanzas that mark much of the work of Langston Hughes and Don Lee is not only naive, but also disappointing. Moreover, to search always for the racial import in the writings of an artist who believed the poet dealt (or, at least, should be able to deal) above the realm of simple earthly distinctions is to find little. To examine the writings of Countee Cullen in detail, however, and attempt to understand both his aesthetic standpoint and the major ideas in his poetry is to move closer to an intelligent interpretation of both the man and the tradition to which he belongs.

The starting point of such an examination is the realization that every notable author in the Black American literary tradition, Cullen included, has been dependent to some extent on the white American literary establishment —that complex of publishers, patrons, critics, scholars, journals, and reviews that can either catapult a writer to success or ignore him. The controversy between Chesnutt and Du Bois over whose biography of John Brown would be allowed to make a profit for the white publisher; Chesnutt's ten-year difficulties surrounding *The House Behind the Cedars;* and Paul Laurence Dunbar's bitter reaction to William Dean Howells's patronizing review of *Lyrics of Lowly Life* offer meet prototypes for today's skirmishes.

Black authors in different sections of the country battle one another to secure rewards from white publishers; apparently neither James Alan McPherson nor Ralph Ellison feels the present atmosphere conducive to a second book; and Ishmael Reed ceaselessly cries forth that critics are unfair to him. When we look beyond the gaudy celebrations of Black creative freedom that deluge today's market, the options available to contemporary Black artists do not seem substantially increased.

The folksinger Odetta says that when she travels throughout the country she is disturbed at the criticism levelled against Black people of talent by other Blacks who feel they are misapplying their gifts; but she concludes that "all roads lead to Rome, and all of them must be covered." A perverse interpretation of this statement reveals its essential truth. Most paths that Black artists have travelled in America *have* led to white economic gains and to the self-congratulation of the white critical establishment. On the title pages of a number of the most highly praised recent Black works, one finds the familiar names—Harper, Doubleday, Harcourt, Bobbs Merrill, etc. Moreover, the sign of success for many Black American writers and critics is acknowledgment by a leading white critic, university, or newspaper.

All of this can be attributed to a system of critics and publishers that goes back to an eighteenth-century British phenomenon. And one can always list such independent Black periodicals and presses as *Black World, Black Books Bulletin,* Third World Press, and Broadside Press. Neither consideration, however, carries one far from the basic premise here: during the past seventy years the situation of the Black American author has remained much the same. His work has been molded largely by the white literary establishment and judged successful or unsuccessful (despite, in some instances, the vehement dissent of Black America) according to the prevailing white critical standards. Any critical theory of Black art that makes a one-to-one correlation between social or propagandistic art and meaningful social gains, therefore, seems absurd.

20

Is it not possible the establishment has simply given us outworn codes and formulas and a few minor concessions? These not only provide an escape valve for energy that might be directed against the larger society—like that released in the ghetto riots of the sixties and the Black institution building of the seventies—but also produce a confusion of aims and an immature refllection on art that result in unenlightening criticism. In this context, one might question why the collected poetry of Langston Hughes has not appeared, while his Simple books, *Not Without Laughter,* and seductive titles such as *The Ways of White Folks, The Sweet Flypaper of Life,* and *The Panther and the Lash* are easily available. One would certainly want to know why Wallace Thurman's *Infants of the Spring* is not well advertised and accessible. And it is relevant to ask why there has been no reissue of the works of Countee Cullen. There seems but one possible answer: our literary tradition, like the rest of our lives, has been and is still controlled by whites to a greater extent than most are willing to admit.

Several critics who have read the books of Countee Cullen have been so confused by this situation that they have failed to provide adequate accounts of the man and his poetry. To state this, however, is not to imply there is no insightful and productive criticism available. Indeed, such work is an integral part of the discussion that follows.

II

Countee Cullen (né Porter) was reared by his grandmother until he was eleven years old; when she died, he was adopted by Reverend Frederick Asbury Cullen, the pastor of Harlem's Salem Methodist Episcopal Church. The boy was given a room to himself in the quiet parsonage; and a new life of books, discussions, and parental tenderness began. The Cullens tended to overindulge their only child, but their kindness, position in the community, and trips to summer places in New Jersey and Maryland did not spoil Cullen for hard work. In both junior and senior high school, the boy was a model student, participating eagerly in extracurricular activities and bringing home commendable marks. In some ways, the adolescence of Cullen reminds one of the early life of the English poet Ernest Dowson. Like Dowson's, his summers were filled with long sheafs of verses describing his activities, and his home was characterized by a respectable frugality and industriousness. Certainly, there was nothing of the pinched and nomadic wandering that beset the life of Langston Hughes. Cullen was exactly the correct young man to enter the somewhat idyllic life of Reverend and Mrs. Cullen. And it is not surprising that stories of lynchings sometimes made him physically ill or that fame early sought him out.

His first published poem, "To the Swimmer," appeared in *The Modern School* during his sophomore year at De Witt Clinton High School, and later "I Have a Rendezvous with Life (with apologies to Alan Seeger)" won first prize in a competition sponsored by a women's organization. Throughout his high school career, Cullen contributed to the literary magazine and continued to hone his poetic talent. He read Paul Laurence Dunbar and the British and American Romantic poets and resolved to be a writer.

After graduating from De Witt Clinton, he entered New York University, and here he came of age as a poet. He won prizes in the Witter Bynner and *Crisis* poetry contests, and by 1924, "it seemed that no literary magazine could bear to go to press without a Countee Cullen poem."[9] In the fall of 1925, Cullen entered the M.A. program at Harvard University; he came bearing fame and a Phi Beta Kappa key. During the same year, *Color* was published by Harper and Brothers, and its seventy-odd poems secured the poet's place as a leading figure of the Harlem Renaissance. The acknowledgments page—which contains such exalted names as *The American Mercury, The Bookman, Harper's Magazine, The Nation, the Crisis,* and *Poetry*—reveals Cullen as one of the first Black American poets after Dunbar to gain national celebrity.

The poet journeyed abroad with his father during the summer of 1926 and in the fall of the same year took an editorial job with *Opportunity,* the official organ of the National Urban League. In 1927, Harper released *Caroling Dusk, Copper Sun* and Cullen's rendering of an old ballad, *The Ballad of the Brown Girl,* in single volumes. A number of critics were disappointed by *Copper Sun,* since it did not bear out the promise revealed in *Color,* but Cullen's spirits were high when he read a letter from George Lyman Kittredge describing *The Ballad of the Brown Girl* as the finest literary ballad he had ever read. The year 1928 brought further praise and a Guggenheim Fellowship. More importantly, it marked the year in which Cullen—with much sound and fury, enthusiasm and ado —was married to the daughter of W. E. B. Du Bois. Far from a quiet and seemly affair, Du Bois viewed the marriage of his Yolande to a "New Negro" poet as a symbolic event, a testament to the "beauty and power of a new breed of American Negro." Given the grandiloquent conceptions of Du Bois, it is not surprising that the ceremony was stunning. Nor is it striking that the couple quickly parted to attend their separate lives—Cullen in Paris and Yolande in Baltimore—and within two years firmly divorced. When he arrived in Paris, however, the young poet's prospects seemed bright. He responded as favorably to France as he had two years earlier, became associated with a group of Black American artists (including Eric Walrond and Augusta Savage), and set about satisfying the expectations of the Guggenheim Foundation. Marital troubles intervened, and soon Cullen found them a constant source of distraction. His output grew smaller as his world-view grew more darkly romantic. The Guggenheim years resulted in the publication of *The Black Christ and Other Poems* in 1929 and a return to the Salem Methodist parsonage as a divorced man.

Early in the 1930s—the decade of the Great Depression that ended the Harlem Renaissance—Cullen decided to take a teaching job at Frederick Douglass Junior High School. This post turned into a career. Though *One Way to Heaven* (a novel, 1932) and *The Medea and Some Poems* (1935) both received kind reviews, by the mid-thirties Cullen's days as a serious writer were past. *The Lost Zoo* (1940) and *My Lives and How I Lost Them* (1942) are both children's books; *On These I Stand* (1947)—a collection of poems outlined before his death —contains only six previously unpublished works. Cullen died on January 10, 1946, and on Saturday, January 12, three thousand people attended his funeral at the Salem Methodist Episcopal Church.

Arna Bontemps writes: "Cullen was in many ways an old-fashioned poet. He never ventured very far from the Methodist parsonage in which he grew up in New York. A foster child, drawn into this shelter at an early age, he continued to cherish it gratefully."[10] Although Cullen always returned home to Harlem no matter how far he journeyed, the implications of Bontemps' statement seem questionable; the poet lived in harmony with his adopted parents and is deemed old-fashioned because he never experienced a stage of Freudian revolt. One can see how Cullen would be considered the exception in an age that brought Wallace Thurman, Bontemps himself, and a host of others from all over the country to seek fame and fortune in Harlem. Cullen was already there. Moreover, he was the first to achieve monumental success as an author and to substantially express what many of the Renaissance writers felt. Cullen is old-fashioned, I think, only to the revisionist who feels he must divide the past into neat blocks and firmly ensconce his favorites.

In many ways, the Harlem Renaissance was simply the artistic extension of the socio-political activities of Black Americans during the 1920s. Its end was integration into the mainstream, and its means were not very different from those of white creative artists. Financial success, acknowledgment by literary figures such as H. L. Mencken, Sara Teasdale, and Witter Bynner, and the acclaim of newspapers like the *New York World* and the *Times* were considered worthy rewards by all American authors. Countee Cullen was not out of step with his age when he gratefully received any of these. And unlike a number of Black American authors, Cullen refused to be wooed and won by white patrons. He firmly rejected Carl Van Vechten's offer to secure a publisher for him and steadfastly refused to be channeled into a narrow stream.

Most often criticized is Cullen's choice of the romantic mode and his reliance on a long-standing poetical tradition. And if his detractors stuck to these charges, there would be little conflict. Most, however, go beyond them and assume that, say, Langston Hughes and Jean Toomer were more forthright, "modern," and independent than Cullen. To do so is to forget that the publication of Hughes's first book was contingent upon the kind offices of Vachel Lindsay, and that Toomer was—according to Marjorie Content Toomer—a man who disavowed all allegiance to the Black Renaissance.[12] The artistic independence of the Black author was an implied goal rather than a tangible fact of the Renaissance, and one suspects that Cullen was not the only author who told Hughes that he wanted to be just a writer, not a "Negro" writer.[13]

. . In short, Cullen can be placed in the Harlem Renaissance camp that viewed the Black writer's objective of universal success as one strategy for lessening the great American dilemma. To set this group at one end of the spectrum and another contingent labelled "nationalists" at the opposite end, however, is to simplify our history. The tendency to look toward the highest ideals of American society and to integrate into its common house has always been present in the minority cultures of this nation; and seldom have they contained an articulate, literate group of substantial size to publish opposition to such inclinations. For to obtain the advantage of a hearing, it has always been necessary to filter through the white man's hands, leaving behind much of the fire and independence of youthful spirit. And the men of the Harlem Renaissance were articulate, literate, and published, most having found their way through the sieve of the white world. If we call before the bench Langston Hughes, we find him starting out as a college student, a bohemian poet who turned out funky stanzas to the tune of a Park Avenue patron. Bring up Jean Toomer, and we have a genius who went unacknowledged during his day because he dared to tell the truth about the fundamental ways of Black folks; this situation drove him to mysticism and whiteness. Summon Countee Cullen, and we receive a man who understood better than most the aims of his articulate Black contemporaries. W. E. B. Du Bois wrote: "In a time when it is the vogue to make much of the Negro's aptitude for clownishness or to depict him objectively as a serio-comic figure, it is a fine and praiseworthy act for Mr. Cullen to show through the interpretation of his own subjectivity the inner workings of the Negro soul and mind."[14] And Alain Locke felt the poet blended "the simple with the sophisticated so originally as almost to put the vineyards themselves into his crystal goblets."[15] The final member of that revered Renaissance triumvirate, James Weldon Johnson, said:

> Cullen is a fine and sensitive lyric poet, belonging to the classic line. . . . He never bids for popular favor through the use of bizarre effects either in manner or subject matter. . . . All of his work is laid within the lines of the long-approved English patterns. And by that very gauge a measure of his gifts and powers as a poet may be taken. The old forms come from his hands filled with fresh beauty. A high test for a poet in this blasé age.[16]

Cullen was not destined to go unsung like Toomer nor was he subject to the kind of disillusionment that overtook Hughes. One of the most accomplished literary representatives of a majority point of view, he received both the lavish (and, at times, inordinate) praise and the ironical discomfort that accompany such a position.

With the wisdom of hindsight, one might glance back on Cullen—and the Harlem Renaissance in general—and talk of the myopia of the 1920s. Many Black American artists and critics felt the millenium had arrived. While this was certainly not true, it seems excessively critical to speak of their faulty vision. A view of Cullen's aesthetic statements reveals that one of his chief demands was the freedom of the Black American artist. Like James Weldon Johnson, Cullen was interested in liberating Black American poetry from the shackles of the past and in developing a strong literary tradition. In a 1926 *Crisis* article, he wrote: "I do believe . . . that the Negro has not yet built up a large enough body of sound, healthy race literature to permit him to speculate in abortions and aberrations which other people are all too prone to accept as truly legitimate."[17] This sounds, on the one hand, like a Victorian moralist calling for fresh air and sunshine in art, but it seems, on the other, wise advice to the poets of an era prone to bizarre tangents. A firm tradition could be established only if the writer exercised meet selectivity. Cullen says:

> Let art portray things as they are, no matter what the consequences, no matter who is hurt, is a blind bit of philosophy. There are some things, some truths of Negro life and thought, of Negro inhibitions that all Negroes know, but take no pride in. To broadcast them to the world will but strengthen the bitterness of our enemies, and in some instances turn away the interest of our friends. . . . *Put forward your best foot.*[18]

This enjoinder was not prescriptive, however; unlike Jessie Fauset and others, Cullen did not believe the field of the Black artist should be severely limited. His statement is a call for what all fine art must possess—authorial discretion. The specific subject matter is the choice of the individual artist:

> Must we, willy-nilly, be forced into writing nothing but the old atavistic urges, the more savage and none too beautiful aspects of our lives? May we not chant a hymn to the Sun God if we will, create a bit of phantasy in which not a spiritual or a blues appears, write a tract defending Christianity though its practitioners aid us so little in our argument; in short do, write, create what we will, our only concern being that we do it well and with all the power in us?[19]

This answer to a French critic who chided Cullen for employing classical allusions and Western subject matter sounds somewhat like Ralph Ellison's rejoinders to Irving Howe's "Black Boys and Native Sons." But one must beware of interpreting the response as the bourgeois artist's apology for his subjects and techniques. Cullen never

27

urged Black writers to turn away from the ghettoes of the land and lose themselves in learned epithets:

> The danger to the young Negro writer is not that he will find his aspiration in the Negro slums; I dare say there are as fine characters and as bright dream material there as in the best strata of Negro society, and that is as it should be. Let the young Negro writer, like any artist, find his treasure where his heart lies. If the unfortunate and less favored find an affinity in him, let him surrender himself; only let him not pander to the popular trend of seeing no cleanliness in their squalor, no nobleness in their meanness and no common sense in their ignorance.[20]

There is condescension, but the overriding appeal here is for the saneness of the Black artist in his presentation, regardless of the subject matter.

Given Cullen's views on the liberty and discretion of the Black artist, it is not surprising that he considered artistic diversity a norm in the Black experience:

> The poet writes out of his experience, whether it be personal or vicarious, and as these experiences differ among other poets, so do they differ among Negro poets; for the double obligation of being both Negro and American is not so unified as we are often led to believe. A survey of the work of Negro poets will show that the individual diversifying ego transcends the synthesizing hue.[21]

The poet's reaction to an article by Frank Mott illustrates how strongly he endorsed this point of view:

> Only at his [Mott's] dictum that an author *ought,* by virtue of birth or any other circumstance, be interested solely in any *particular* thing do we utter protest. The mind of man has always ridden a capricious wandering nag, that just will not stay reined into a beaten path. . . . Let us not then be stricken into such dire lamentation when the Negro author goes excursioning. Let the test be how much of a pleasant day he himself has had, and how much he has been enabled to impart to us.[22]

As Cullen points out, however, the Black American's double consciousness does not present a simple problem. Though he made a strong case for the Black artist's freedom from limiting categories (hoping that any merit that might reside in his own works would "flow from it solely as the expression of a poet—with no racial considerations to bolster it up"),[23] he found himself insensibly drawn into writing racial verse. In 1926, he said:

> In spite of myself . . . I find that I am actuated by a strong sense of race consciousness. This grows upon me, I find, as I grow older, and although I struggle against it, it colors my writing, I fear, in spite of everything I can do. There may have been many things in my life that have hurt me, and I find that the surest relief from these hurts is in writing.[24]

And in an interview for the *Chicago Bee* during the following year, he said:

> Most things I write, I do for the sheer love of the music in them. Somehow or other, however, I find my poetry of itself treating of the Negro, of his joys and his sorrows—mostly of the latter, and of the heights and the depths of emotion which I feel as a Negro.[25]

The apologetic tone of these statements is considered gratuitous by our own generation, but in a poet as concerned with widening the horizons of the Black author as Countee Cullen, the sentiments are genuine. Cullen himself wanted to be an accepted poet, and he hoped that his example and advice would lead to the instatement of others in the hall of acknowledged American authors. He realized that from one point of view his task was far from simple:

> This question of what material the Negro writer should draw upon, and how he should use it, is no simon pure problem with a sure mathematical conclusion; it has innumerable ramifications, and almost all arguments can be met with a dissenting *but* equally as strong.[26]

One critic clarifies the reason the question was not "simon pure": "In the twenties the Negro's gifts were still departmentalized. There were poets in the United States, and there were Negro poets."[27] During the 1920s (as today) the "Negro poet" was automatically deemed inferior to "the Poet." It is one thing to say that Cullen should never have fallen prey to such speculations; it is quite another to realize that he was torn by the dichotomy and that in the process of working it out he made some of the strongest statements on Black artistic freedom that emerged from the Harlem Renaissance. His apologies can surely be seen as lamentations that America produced a kind of schizophrenia in the Black artist and made it impossible for him to translate his highest ideals into a unified and consistent body of poetry that would rank with the canons of John Keats and Percy Shelley. Moreover, they can be viewed as his painful realizations that the Black man is often so scarred by his experiences in America that it is difficult for him to sustain the romantic point of view that Cullen felt most conducive to poetry. The question here is not disillusionment, but having all roads blocked from the outset. A careful reading of Cullen's aesthetic dictates reveals a man with his mind set on freedom, but one who—like the creatures in George Orwell's *Animal Farm* or like Ellison's protagonist in *Invisible Man*—was confused by the relativity of the term. The inconsistency of Cullen's canon—its peaks and deep valleys—is understandable within this context. A fine, militant racial poem is sometimes followed by popularistic verse urging a hedonistic Black existence, and skillful lyrics detailing the beauty of spring precede the most trite and unimaginative stanzas on despair. Cullen was certain that he did not want to be hemmed in—that he wanted to be accepted as just a poet—but he was not sure what constituted the most daring and accomplished freedom for an American author who happened to be Black. Johnson succinctly captures his situation:

> The colored poet in the United States labors within limitations which he cannot easily pass over. He is always on the defensive or the offensive. The pressure upon him to be propagandic is well nigh irresistible. These conditions are suffocating to breadth and to real art in poetry. In addition he labors under the handicap of finding culture not entirely colorless in the United States.[28]

III

In a headnote in *Caroling Dusk,* Cullen states that one of his chief problems was "reconciling a Christian upbringing with a pagan inclination."[29] The poems in *Color* reveal the accuracy of his comment, for a dichotomy pervades the volume. Faith and doubt, hedonism and reverence, innocence and experience, white and black, life and death are constantly juxtaposed, and the tensions that result often lead to striking poems. In the dedicatory poem, for example, the brevity of existence is set against the implied immortality of the poet, and the germination of spring is seen as a foil for the destructiveness of winter:

> When the dreadful Ax
> Rives me apart,
> When the sharp wedge cracks
> My arid heart,
> Turn to this book
> Of the singing me
> For a springtime look
> At the wintry tree.[30]

And in "Tableau," Cullen uses nature imagery to demonstrate the contrast between black and white, the natural and the artificial:

> Locked arm in arm they cross the way,
> The black boy and the white,
> The golden splendor of the day,
> The sable pride of night.
>
> From lowered blinds the dark folk stare,
> And here the fair folk talk,
> Indignant that these two should dare
> In unison to walk.

The boys are outside, joined in the natural camaraderie of youth, while their elders—both Black and white—gossip about their friendship behind lowered blinds. Bertram Woodruff has commented aptly on the bifurcation in Cullen's poetry between a cynical realism and a subjective idealism—a materialistic and a theistic conception of life[31] —and James Weldon Johnson noted the poet's sudden ironic turns of thought.[32] These are essential characteristics of the canon and grow, in part, out of the conflicts occasioned by Cullen's aesthetic stance. The poet who did not want his work bolstered by racial considerations begins

31

Color with twenty-four racial poems. The artist who adopted the romantic mode is pulled continually toward the darker side of this realm, and his work abounds in pessimism and despair. Divided into four sections—Color, Epitaphs, For Love's Sake, and Varia—*Color* expresses the major themes of the canon.

The racial poems in the volume range from the somewhat bombastic "The Shroud of Color" to the magnificently sustained and accomplished "Heritage" with a variety of noble sentiment, libertinism, atavism, fine description, and "initiation" filling out the middle range. Arthur Davis has demonstrated that one of the chief subjects of the opening section is alienation and exile:

> For Cullen, the Negro is both a geographical and a spiritual exile. He has lost not only an idyllic homeland; but equally as important, he has also lost understanding pagan gods who would be far more sympathetic to his peculiar needs than the pale Christian deities.[33]

One finds this sense of displacement in poems such as "Atlantic City Waiter," "Near White," "Brown Boy to Brown Girl," "Pagan Prayer," and "Heritage." In these poems, the Black man is conceived as a deracinated individual pulled abruptly from some edenic place and set amidst strange gods. But there are also poems that show no sense of alienation; they simply enjoin a hedonistic existence. "To a Brown Girl," for example, offers the following comment:

> What if his glance is bold and free,
>   His mouth the lash of whips?
> So should the eyes of lovers be,
>   And so a lover's lips.

And "To a Brown Boy" gives similar advice:

> That brown girl's swagger gives a twitch
>   To beauty like a queen;
> Lad, never dam your body's itch
>   When loveliness is seen.

There are poems, moreover, that have more to do with a specific social situation than with a feeling of exile. "A

Brown Girl Dead" and "Saturday's Child" are both ironical protests against economic oppression:

> Her mother pawned her wedding ring
> To lay her out in white;
> She'd be so proud she'd dance and sing
> To see herself tonight.
> ("A Brown Girl Dead")

> For I was born on Saturday—
> "Bad time for planting a seed,"
> Was all my father had to say,
> And, "One mouth more to feed."

> Death cut the strings that gave me life,
> And handed me to Sorrow,
> The only kind of middle wife
> My folks could beg or borrow.
> ("Saturday's Child")

The dominant feeling of the racial poems, however, is (in the words of Claude McKay) one of being "born, far from my native clime,/Under the white man's menace, out of time."

"Yet Do I Marvel" and "Heritage" capture the irony and ambiguity of this situation. The former is devastating in its restrained cynicism:

> I doubt not God is good, well-meaning, kind,
> And did He stoop to quibble could tell why
> The little buried mole continues blind,
> Why flesh that mirrors Him must some day die.

The list of incongruities moves to the assertion that God's ways are too grandiose for the simple human mind; then with a swift stroke of genius, come the concluding lines:

> Yet do I marvel at this curious thing:
> To make a poet black, and bid him sing!

The *angst* of Cullen's aesthetic is summed up in this couplet. By association, the Black poet takes on the burdens of the disinherited and is doomed to the tortures of Sisyphus and Tantalus; the persona exposes both his own skepticism and the awesome task of the Black artist.

33

"Heritage" displays the same sense of irony and skepticism. The poem opens with what turns out to be a rhetorical question:

> What is Africa to me:
> Copper sun or scarlet sea,
> Jungle star or jungle track,
> Strong bronzed men, or regal black
> Women from whose loins I sprang
> When the birds of Eden sang?

The text reveals that Africa is not only the spirit realm to which the narrator feels most allied, but also a land in fierce opposition to his present home. As in McKay's "Flame-Heart," the narrator of "Heritage" makes a claim that is not justified by the poem itself:

> Africa? A book one thumbs
> Listlessly, till slumber comes.
> Unremembered are her bats
> Circling through the night, her cats
> Crouching in the river reeds,
> Stalking gentle flesh that feeds
> By the river brink. . . .

The vivid descriptions of its fierce flowers and pagan impulses show that Africa is much more than bedtime reading for the narrator. Moreover, when he states that he is trying to move beyond the call of heathen deities, the text leaps forth in refutation. Some critics have faulted Cullen for "Heritage," stating that he makes topographical mistakes and perpetuates the idea of the Black man as a "noble savage."[34] Such responses can carry one only so far, however, with a poem as thoroughly ironical as "Heritage." While it is true that there is an undue enthusiasm recurrent in the passages on Africa, it is also true that Cullen was interested in a blatant contrast between the benign and unsmiling deities of the new land and the thoroughly initiated gods of the old. The entire poem is placed in a confessional framework as the narrator tries to define his relationship to some white, ontological being and finds that a Black impulse ceaselessly draws him back. The

34

italicized concluding lines read like the penance exacted from an unregenerate schoolboy:

> *All day long and all night through,*
> *One thing only must I do:*
> *Quench my pride and cool my blood,*
> *Lest I perish in the flood,*
> *Lest a hidden ember set*
> *Timber that I thought was wet*
> *Burning like the dryest flax,*
> *Melting like the merest wax,*
> *Lest the grave restore its dead.*
> *Not yet has my heart or head*
> *In the least way realized*
> *They and I are civilized.*

"Heritage" is a longer and more comprehensive statement of the message contained in "Pagan Prayer," and it reveals the sharp line that Cullen saw dividing two cultures. The poet's "paganism" reveals itself in the end as a repudiation of the white man's religion.

A poem like "Incident" reveals why such a rejection is necessary:

> Once riding in old Baltimore,
>   Heart-filled, head-filled with glee,
> I saw a Baltimorean
>   Keep looking straight at me.
>
> Now I was eight and very small,
>   And he was no whit bigger,
> And so I smiled, but he poked out
>   His tongue, and called me, "Nigger."
>
> I saw the whole of Baltimore
> From May until December;
> Of all the things that happened there
>   That's all that I remember.

The sense of irony and the dichotomized world-view that appear throughout Cullen's work are skillfully captured here. There is a movement from gay innocence to initiation,[35] which is repeated in the seasonal reference ("May until December"), and at the time of recounting the speaker has not forgotten the incident. Not only the vistas of Baltimore, one suspects, but the whole of his life has been clouded by the sudden realization that the norms of the larger society do not work for him. Adjustment often involves the type of repudiation seen in "Heritage" and "Pagan Prayer."

The two themes that stand out in *Color's* nonracial poems are love and mortality. The second section consists of twenty-nine epitaphs written in the manner of Edgar Lee Master's *Spoon River Anthology*. Cullen, however, is not interested in showing what the restrictions of the village do to the human psyche. He is concerned with the many types that make up society, and thus the poems display subtle irony, tender feeling, and adept portraiture. "For a Lady I Know" captures in miniature the type of woman whom the poet's atavistic "Atlantic City Waiter" might have served:

> She even thinks that up in heaven
> Her class lies late and snores,
> While poor black cherubs rise at seven
> To do celestial chores.

"For My Grandmother" demonstrates Cullen's ability to set forth mild sentiments:

> This lovely flower fell to seed;
> Work gently, sun and rain;
> She held it as her dying creed
> That she would grow again.

There is fine irony in both "For a Virgin" and "For an Atheist":

> For forty years I shunned the lust
> Inherent in my clay;
> Death only was so amorous
> I let him have his way.

and

> Mountains cover me like rain,
> Billows whirl and rise;
> Hide me from the stabbing pain
> In His reproachful eyes.

Finally, there is the often quoted "For Paul Laurence Dunbar":

> Born of the sorrowful of heart,
>   Mirth was a crown upon his head;
> Pride kept his twisted lips apart
>   In jest, to hide a heart that bled.

Though the poems as a group offer a comment on various styles of human life, the overwhelming fact of the sequence —as of all epitaphs—is the common end to which flesh is heir. This condition brings about much of the humor that resides in the individual sketches, and the same sense of mortality occasions the despair that appears in a number of the poems in the concluding sections of *Color*.

It may seem commonplace to say that Cullen's romanticism is derivative, but in the context of nineteenth-century English poetry, the statement becomes more descriptive. Though the poet chose as his ideal the second wave of British romanticism, including Keats and Shelley, his own lyrics read more like the work of Dante Rossetti, Charles Swinburne, and the authors of *fin de siécle* England. These were the romantics *manqué* who shared the same lyrical impulses but lacked the sweeping vision, the mythicizing potential, and the colossal certainties of their predecessors. The shades of Ernest Dowson and Arthur Symons appear with the first lines of "Oh, For a Little While Be Kind":

> Oh, for a little while be kind to me
> Who stand in such imperious need of you,
> And for a fitful space let my head lie
> Happily on your passion's frigid breast.

The moment of contentment is brief, and though the poem ends on an ironical note, its basic assumptions are that life is fleeting and love is short. "If You Should Go" deals once again with the departure of the beloved, and "To One Who Said Me Nay" is a restatement of the familiar *carpe diem* theme. "Advice to Youth" follows the same pattern, while "Caprice" captures the heart-rending and incomprehensible ways of love:

> "I'll tell him, when he comes," she said,
>   "Body and baggage, to go,
> Though the night be darker than my hair,
>   And the ground be hard with snow."

> But when he came with his gay black head
>   Thrown back, and his lips apart,
> She flipped a light hair from his coat,
>   And sobbed against his heart.

The male figure here reminds one of the protagonist in "Two Who Crossed a Line (He Crosses)," and once again we see the contrasts that mark Cullen's verse—harmony and discontent, light and dark. Both "Sacrament" and "Bread and Wine"—as one might expect—juxtapose the sacred and the profane. In the first, the speaker is considered unworthy of the beloved; in the second, the beloved is deemed the only thing holy in a mortal world. Cullen's use of religious imagery in the two poems is in harmony with his canon as a whole, for time and again there are biblical allusions.[36] The final poem in the third section, "Spring Reminiscence," moves quite well until the final couplet, where the merger of a religious allusion with a colloquialism destroys the effect. The poem, however, has thematic significance, for it is a memory in spring of springs gone by. There is the possibility, in other words, of resurrecting the joy and beauty of the past through the agency of poetry. The poet and his experiences possess a certain immortality, and spring—the time of nature's rejuvenation —becomes symbolic of enduring spirituality.

All of this cannot be inferred from "Spring Reminiscence," of course, but the stanza quoted earlier from "To You Who Read My Book," combined with "In Memory of Col. Charles Young" and "To John Keats, Poet. At Springtime," make the argument clearer. Young, the Black colonel who was retired from the army at the beginning of World War I to prevent his promotion to general, becomes one with nature in the course of the poem:

> The great dark heart is like a well
>   Drained bitter by the sky,
> And all the honeyed lies they tell
>   Come there to thirst and die.

> No lie is strong enough to kill
> The roots that work below;
> From your rich dust and slaughtered will
> A tree with tongues will grow.

And there is a similar merger and generative process in "To
John Keats, Poet. At Springtime":

> And you and I, shall we lie still,
> John Keats, while Beauty summons us?
> Somehow I feel your sensitive will
> Is pulsing up some tremulous
> Sap road of a maple tree, whose leaves
> Grow music as they grow, since your
> Wild voice is in them, a harp that grieves
> For life that opens death's dark door.
> Though dust, your fingers still can push
> The Vision Splendid to a birth,
> Though now they work as grass in the hush
> Of the night on the broad sweet page of the earth.

Part of Cullen's "pagan inclination" displays itself in poems
like these, where he not only reminds us of the ineluct-
ability of the spiritual, but also recalls the fact that spring
(before its arrogation by Christianity) was a time of bac-
chanalian celebration and heady splendor in the grass. For
the poet, spring is the season when the natural man, the
sensitive soul, and the germinating seed push forth in a re-
birth of wonder.

Finally in *Color* are Cullen's concern for the outcast—
"Black Magdalens," "For Daughters of Magdalen," and
"Judas Iscariot"—and his treatment of the idealistic dreamer. The poet achieves a masterful irony by placing street-
walkers in a biblical context:

> They fare full ill since Christ forsook
> The cross to mount a throne,
> And Virtue still is stooping down
> To cast the first hard stone.

and

> Ours is the ancient story:
> Delicate flowers of sin,
> Lilies, arrayed in glory,
> That would not toil nor spin.

Judas is viewed as a man who had to betray Christ so the vision He cherished would come true. In "Simon the Cyrenian Speaks," the persona says:

> But He was dying for a dream,
> And He was very meek,
> And in His eyes there shone a gleam
> Men journeyed far to seek.

In "For a Poet," the creative artist is also viewed as a keeper of dreams. Like other matter in Cullen's canon, therefore, Christianity is seen in a dual light. Insofar as God is cryptic or inscrutable in *Color's* first two poems, He is the object of cynicism and repudiation; as Christ, the carrier of the dream, however, He is to be ranked among the highest idealists.

"I've kept on doing the same things, and doing them no better. I have never gotten to the things I really wanted to do," Dunbar told James Weldon Johnson as he suffered the agonies of his final illness.[37] Some would expect a similar confession from Countee Cullen, since *Color* is his finest volume, although he went on to produce four more. If the poet had made a similar statement, he would have falsified his own accomplishments. Some things he did a good deal better as his career progressed. From his early efforts, he moved to the fine group of poems labelled "Interlude" in *The Black Christ,* and he developed his narrative voice in *The Ballad of the Brown Girl.* He not only provided a rendering of Euripides's *Medea,* but also did work as a translator. And in his final volume, he seems to counteract—through the sanity and balance of his verse—Benjamin Brawley's charge that "there is a sophomoric note in the work of Mr. Cullen that he finds it hard to outgrow."[38]

The overriding dichotomy in the second volume is one of stasis and change. On the one hand, the poet believes despair is enduring and death the bitter end of all. On the other, he sees a better day approaching, the possibility of regeneration and immortality, and death as an occasion for solace and wisdom. The seven racial poems in *Copper*

40

Sun[39] fall generally on the positive side. Though he is now battered and scarred, there is a new day coming for the Black American:

> We shall not always plant while others reap
> The golden increment of bursting fruit,
> Not always countenance, abject and mute,
> That lesser men should hold their brothers cheap
>   ("From the Dark Tower")

> If for a day joy masters me,
> Think not my wounds are healed;
> . . . .
> They shall bear blossoms with the fall;
> I have their word for this,
> Who tend my roots with rains of gall,
> And suns of prejudice.
>   ("Confession")

> Our flesh that was a battle-ground
> Shows now the morning-break;
> The ancient deities are downed
> For Thy eternal sake.
> Now that the past is left behind,
> Fling wide Thy garment's hem
> To keep us one with Thee in mind,
> Thou Christ of Bethlehem.
>   ("The Litany of the Dark People")

The metaphor of germination appears (particularly in "Threnody for a Brown Girl"), and the last poem in the group seems to favor an acceptance of the white man's religion as a means of salvation. Despite the laconic warning of Uncle Jim that "White folks is white," the speaker in most of the poems has adopted the attitude that improvement is a reality for the Black American. There are tones of apocalypse in both "From the Dark Tower" and "Confession," but "The Litany of the Dark People" does much to soften them.

The optimism of the first section is out of harmony with the remainder of *Copper Sun,* for a note of despondency sounds with "Pity the Deep in Love." And while there is a contrapuntal rhythm between this and the poems

that speak of the eternality of beauty and the splendor of
the dream, the pervasive timbre is melancholy:

> Pity the deep in love;
> They move as men asleep,
> Traveling a narrow way
> Precipitous and steep.
>> ("Pity the Deep in Love"))

> But never past the frail intent
> My will may flow,
> Though gentle looks of yours are bent
> Upon me where I go.

> So must I, starved for love's delight,
> Affect the mute,
> When love's divinest acolyte
> Extends me holy fruit.
>> ("Timid Lover")

> Of all men born he deems himself so much accurst,
> His plight so piteous, his proper pain so rare,
> The very bread he eats so dry, so fierce his thirst,
> What shall we liken such a martyr to? Compare
> Him to a man with poison raging in his throat,
> And far away the one mind with an antidote.
>> ("Portrait of a Lover")

The unrequited love, dejection, indifference, *carpe diem,*
and sighing in *Copper Sun* would have delighted the nineteenth-century decadent poets and would stimulate anew
the pale shades of Sir John Suckling and Edmund Waller.
Cullen's songs of desperation in the second volume do not
seem to have a substantial base; somehow they come across
as exercises in depression rather than genuine reflections
of the poet's inner being. It is, of course, difficult to argue
about the effect a poem has on the reader, and one should
steer clear of Wimsatt and Beardsley's "affective fallacy"—
contemplating a poem as though it were the ground for
some ultimate emotional state.[40] What heightens one's
impression of insincerity, however, is the body of poems
that state exactly the opposite point of view.

The lovers' relationship may not terminate entirely,
and there is always a nagging hope in the background:

42

> What if you come
> Again and swell
> The throat of some
> Mute bird;
> How shall I tell?
> How shall I know
> That it is so,
> Having heard?
>
> ("Words to My Love")

> Come, let us plant our love as farmers plant
> A seed, and you shall water it with tears,
> And I shall weed it with my hands until
> They bleed. Perchance this buried love of ours
> Will fall on goodly ground and bear a tree
> With fruit and flowers . . .
>
> ("The Love Tree")

Though love departs, its beauty may either linger or be reborn. And this ambiguity is also present in the poet's treatment of death, for in "To Lovers of Earth: Fair Warning" he states that man's end is certain and that it goes unmarked by nature. In the following poem, "In Spite of Death," however, the speaker says:

> No less shall I in some new fashion flare
> Again, when death has blown my candles out;
> Although my blood went down in shameful rout
> Tonight, by all this living frame holds fair,
> Though death should closet me tonight, I swear
> Tomorrow's sun would find his cupboard bare.

In "Cor Cordium," "The Poet," and "To Endymion," Cullen once again views the poet and his song as immortal and further confuses the issue with "Hunger" and "At the Wailing Wall in Jerusalem," where he views both dreams and the holy wall as tokens of everlasting beauty.

The question is not one of arrangement in *Copper Sun;* no new scheme would alter the content of the individual poems. Cullen seems to have been confronted with the problem of choosing between alternatives. The smaller number of racial poems is an indication that he had decided to steer closer to the universal romantic ideal, but the prevailing dichotomy and the issue of "belief in poetry" that it raises give evidence that he had not found a firm base on which to stand as a romantic poet. He laments, derides, and protests the passing of love and life but never faces the issues of despair and mortality in a convincing manner. One suspects that Harvey Webster had *Copper Sun* very much in mind when he wrote: "Cullen neither accepted nor developed a comprehensive world-view. As a consequence his poems seem to result from occasional impulses rather than from directions by an integrated individual."[41] Of course, one knows that Cullen was anything but an "integrated individual" and that the bifurcations in his *Weltanschauung* result, in part, from his aesthetic stance. They play an important role in *Color*. In the second volume, however, the division between stasis and change is accompanied by a narrowing of range and blatant contradictions that cause one to think back on Brawley's statement with a smile of assent.

The Ballad of the Brown Girl, An Old Ballad Retold[42] makes much more effective use of the divisions that are basic to Cullen's poetry. The narrator insists that the story was garnered from the grandams "in the land where the grass is blue," and it is not surprising that an English ballad should find its way into the repertoire of a Kentucky storyteller, since some regions of that state were at one time considered the finest preserves of British Elizabethan dialect. What is striking is the interpretation that Cullen places on the ballad. Rather than a story of a "dark brown" peasant contending with a fair city maiden for the heart of an aristocrat, the story is presented as a small and colorful drama of miscegenation and conflict. The leitmotif and moral involve the dangers of the acquisitive instincts, and Lord Thomas's mother is left with the burden of the guilt. Cullen shows himself a master of the ballad stanza in the poem, and his unique rendering of the tale makes it possible for him to engage in fine color imagery:

> Her hair was black as sin is black
> And ringed about with fire;
> Her eyes were black as night is black
> When moon and stars conspire;

> Her mouth was one red cherry clipt
> In twain, her voice a lyre.

or

> Her skin was white as almond milk
> Slow trickling from the flower;
> Her frost-blue eyes were darkening
> Like clouds before a shower.

There are several things that mar the poem. First, the hero is a pale and nervous spectre when the ballad opens, a man who must kneel before his mother to learn which woman to choose. At the end, he is a farseeing individual capable of an ennobling suicide. T. S. Eliot's reservations about Hamlet might well apply to Lord Thomas. Second, Cullen—after a skillful dramatic buildup and climax—relies upon description for his denouement. Finally, the ascription of guilt to the mother seems simplistic, as do the morals of most ballads. Cullen could have mined his material, however, for a more complex statement of the issues his interpretation raises. There are also several infelicities of style.

The Black Christ and Other Poems[43] represents a marked progression in Cullen's thought. The volume closes rather than opens with a section titled "Color," and the beginning "Varia" group makes a number of definite statements about the poet and the age in which he lives. In "To the Three for Whom the Book," the speaker is the committed, romantic poet—the man who dwells above the bending of an "idolatrous knee" to stone and steel. He is the individual who writes of "old, unhappy, far-off things, /And battles long ago." "That Bright Chimeric Beast" reinforces the point:

> That bright chimeric beast
> Conceived yet never born,
> Save in the poet's breast,
> The white-flanked unicorn,
> Never may be shaken
> From his solitude;
> Never may be taken
> In any earthly wood.

There is lost love and despondency in *The Black Christ,*

but the volume also expresses a sincerity and a certainty about the artist's task that are lacking in *Copper Sun*. In "To an Unknown Poet," the dreamer is removed from an unholy time, and in "Counter Mood," the speaker asserts his own immortality. "A Miracle Demanded" comes as a surprise from the poet who marched to a pagan drummer in *Color;* he now asks for a renewal of his faith and a confirmation of the position taken in "Counter Mood." Finally, there are poems like "A Wish," "Minutely Hurt," and "Self Criticism" that show a movement toward a more balanced view of life. In "Minutely Hurt," there is little of the dire lamentation of the rejected lover, and the other two poems express the poet's hope that when he has had his say he will possess the wisdom and courage to stop writing. Meanwhile, the dreamer's life remains one of commitment and loneliness:

> The poet is compelled to love his star,
> Not knowing he could never tell you why
> Though silence makes inadequate reply.
>
> ("Tongue-tied")

> A hungry cancer will not let him rest
> Whose heart is loyal to the least of dreams;
> There is a thorn forever in his breast
> Who cannot take his world for what it seems;
> Aloof and lonely must he ever walk,
> Plying a strange and unaccustomed tongue,
> An alien to the daily round of talk,
> Mute when the sordid songs of earth are sung.
>
> ("A Thorn Forever in the Breast")

The sense of maturity and dedication in *The Black Christ* results first, from the marital difficulties Cullen was encountering when a number of the poems were written. Second, the volume was composed in France, and it is possible that Cullen felt he could be "just a poet" there:

> As he whose eyes are gouged craves light to see,
> And he whose limbs are broken strength to run,
> So have I sought in you that alchemy
> That knits my bones and turns me to the sun;
> And found across a continent of foam
> What was denied my hungry heart at home.
>
> ("To France," from *The Medea and Some Poems*)

46

Third, when *The Black Christ* was published, he had tentatively resolved the problem of a Christian background and a pagan inclination.

"Interlude," the section that deals with the termination of a love affair, constitutes one of the most unified and consistent groups of Cullen's poetry, and its careful style and unfeigned simplicity are akin to George Meredith's *Modern Love*. Two poems capture the spirit and the mastery of the group:

> I know of all the words I speak or write,
> Precious and woven of a vibrant sound,
> None ever snares your faith, intrigues you quite,
> Or sends you soaring from the solid ground.
> You are the level-headed lover who
> Can match my fever while the kisses last,
> But you are never shaken through and through;
> Your roots are firm after the storm has passed.
>
> I shall know nights of tossing in my sleep
> Fondling a hollow where a head should lie;
> But you a calm review, no tears to weep,
> No wounds to dress, no futile breaths to sigh.
> Ever this was the way of wind with flame:
> To harry it, then leave swift as it came.
>
> ("The Simple Truth")

> Breast under breast when you shall lie
>   With him who in my place
> Bends over you with flashing eye
>   And ever nearing face;
>
> Hand fast in hand when you shall tread
>   With him the springing ways
> Of love from me inherited
>   After my little phase;
>
> Be not surprised if suddenly
>   The couch of air confound
> Your ravished ears upbraidingly,
>   And silence turn to sound.
>
> But never let it trouble you,
>   Or cost you one caress;
> Ghosts are soon sent with a word or two
>   Back to their loneliness.
>
> ("Ghosts")

47

Cullen thus deals with the most genuine and heart-rending emotions he had ever felt, and in the volume's final poem he constructs his strongest assertion of faith.

"The Black Christ (Hopefully dedicated to White America)" is the story of a lynching in which Christ mysteriously appears and offers himself for the intended victim. The poem traces the narrator's movement from doubt to faith and depicts his mother as an archetypal southern Black American who holds to the ideals of Christianity. To view the poem as simply the story of a rebellious and agnostic Jim who strikes down a white man and is condemned to death by a mob, however, is to do it less than justice. And, in a sense, to treat the poem as a simple resolution of the narrator's uncertainties is to fail to comprehend its significance in Cullen's canon. On its most fundamental level, "The Black Christ" fits into the tradition of Black American literature as a conversion tale; it is one of those recountings—complete with mysterious events and marvellings at the Lord's way—that characterized the Black church during Reconstruction and that can be heard today when the out-of-town guest is called upon to "testify." Cullen captures the spirit of these occasions quite well in *One Way to Heaven,* and there is little doubt that the son of a successful Harlem minister was familiar with conversion stories. If the poem is seen in this light, some of its apparent flaws turn out to be necessities, e.g., the long retelling of incidents and the sense of suspense and wonder the narrator attempts to create toward the conclusion. A man speaking to a congregation would not be remiss in accounting for every detail and strange phenomenon.

Cullen seems to adopt the form of the conversion story in a rather tentative way, however, for Jim—the agnostic badman hero—certainly appears as glamorous as the sacrificial Christ. But surely this was intentional, since the final reconciliation represents a momentary stasis in the Christian-pagan conflict. Jim, after all, commits his assault because the white man has corrupted the natural reverence for spring on the part of the Black man and white woman, and the virginal tree on which Christ is hung comes to life

48

after the lynching. Christ (the representative of religious faith) and Jim—the sensitive, agnostic worshipper of spring—come together in a rite of regeneration. In the pagan and natural moment, Jim and the white woman are as harmonious as the boys in "Tableau." The white man intrudes, and he and the mob stand for white America. The narrator never loses his admiration for his brother, and the wonder and firmness he feels in his new faith are the results of a miracle.

Throughout the poem, Cullen seems to stand by the narrator's side, whispering that both Christ, the dreamer, and the pagan-spirited Jim are needed to unify the opposing points of his canon. To say the poet avoids some of the issues—like Christ's exoneration of a murderer and the hopelessness His crucifixion portends—is to capture the letter of the poem, but not its spirit. It was inevitable that Cullen would attempt a synthesis and that he would do so in a manner that raised the question of race. The results are not altogether satisfactory, but the strong commitment to an idealistic point of view should not be forgotten. The poet, the dreamer, the man who treasures the wonders of spring wins out in the end. If culture was not entirely "colorless" in the United States, at least it was neutral enough in France for Cullen to compose his only truly romantic volume of poetry. The book contains the poet's message "To Certain Critics":

> Then call me traitor if you must,
> Shout treason and default!
> Say I betray a sacred trust
> Aching beyond this vault.
> I'll bear your censure as your praise,
> For never shall the clan
> Confine my singing to its way
> Beyond the ways of man.
>
> No racial option narrows grief,
> Pain is no patriot,
> And sorrow plaits her dismal leaf
> For all as lief as not.
> With blind sheep groping every hill,
> Searching an oriflamme,

How shall the shepherd heart then thrill
To only the darker lamb?

Six years elapsed between *The Black Christ* and *The Medea and Some Poems,*[44] Cullen's last volume of serious verse. The prose rendering of Euripides's classic play is interesting and shows a broadening of the poet's activities, but it possesses little of the grandeur of the original. Cullen added two female characters to the drama to act as confidantes for Medea; in Euripides's version, the entire chorus acts the role. The substitution means that one of the Greek dramatist's major contentions loses much of its force; no longer is a large sector of the city-state inclined toward the irrationality and paganism represented by the heroine. There seems little possibility that the entire order will be destroyed by the kind of wild frenzy that characterizes the *Bacchae.* Cullen's work is also more maudlin than Euripides's. Medea's soliloquy over her victims and the words of one of her children before the execution—"What are you such a baby for? Mother won't hurt us. Ah!"—drip with sentimentality. Finally, Cullen's characters speak far too often in Poor-Richard slang, and his heroine is reduced to a shrew who engages in such incongruously comical exchanges as:

Medea: Then you have no sons yet, Aegeus?
Aegeus: None. The gods have kept me barren!
Medea: Have you tried a wife? That might help.

Cullen's effort precedes Jean Paul Sartre's rendition of Aeschylus by a number of years. But Sartre's *The Flies* was undertaken as an act of freedom and was first performed in occupied Paris. Hence, there is more justification for his deliberately second-rate translation; it offers an example of "engaged" literature. Cullen's play suffers by comparison, for it shifts the original emphasis on the mythic, barbarian, and fatalistic to the hard-hearted woman scorned. Certainly, this aspect is present in the Euripidean version, but it is not blatant. Cullen's flaccid prose and rhyming choruses are scarcely improvements on earlier translations.

The twenty-eight lyrics in *The Medea* make the volume readable and show a mellowing of the poet's attitudes and a refinement of his technique. There is an expansion of his humanism in verses such as "Magnets," "Any Human to Another," "Every Lover," and "To One Not There," and he rededicates himself to poetry in "After a Visit (At Padraic Colum's where there were Irish poets)." His sonnet "Some for a little while do love" and the concluding poems of *The Medea* show a movement toward a more controlled verse and a more gentle (one might almost say "senescent") point of view:

> Some for a little while do love, and some for long;
> And some rare few forever and for aye;
> Some for the measure of a poet's song,
> And some the ribbon width of a summer's day.
> Some on a golden crucifix do swear,
> And some in blood do plight a fickle troth;
> Some struck divinely mad may only stare,
> And out of silence weave an iron oath.
>
> So many ways love has none may appear
> The bitter best, and none the sweetest worst;
> Strange food the hungry have been known to bear,
> And brackish water slakes an utter thirst.
> It is a rare and tantalizing fruit
> Our hands reach for, but nothing absolute.

"To France" asks that the land of "kindly foreign folk" act as the poet's Byzantium, and "Belitis Sings (From the French of Pierre Louys)" is charming in its delicate artificiality. Finally, "The Cat" and "Cats"—both translations of Baudelaire—substitute the feline loveliness of a domestic pet for the mythical beasts and fickle lovers seen elsewhere in Cullen's canon. Cats are "quiet as scholars and as lovers bold," and they sit "in noble attitudes" and dream —"small sphinxes miming those in lonelier lands." The poet thus sinks quietly into a land of domesticity with a cat for his companion.

The volume closes, however, with "Scottsboro, Too, Is Worth Its Song," a protest poem on the order of "Not Sacco and Vanzetti" *(The Black Christ).* Though Cullen

51

would, henceforth, live and write in collaboration with his cherished Christopher Cat, "all disgrace" and "epic wrong" still exercise their ineluctable and dichotomizing influence. The man who was born Black and bidden to sing turned to the world of children for his next two books, but his canon closes on the propagandistic note that James Weldon Johnson found "well nigh irresistible" for the Black artist.

IV

Countee Cullen never achieved the "Vision Splendid." He can be classified as a minor poet whose life and poetry raise major problems. If we condemn him for his lack of independence and his rise to fame through the agency of noted American critics and periodicals, we are forced to do the same for a host of others. If he is judged and sentenced to exile on the basis of his aesthetic, a number of excellent statements on the Black artist's tasks and difficulties are lost. If he is upbraided for his lack of directness and his reliance on a longstanding tradition, our evaluation of the entire corpus of Black American poetry must be modified. It is possible that we are now whirling about fiercely in the maelstrom of a Black poetic revolution, but a careful view of Countee Cullen brings doubt. There is much continuity between the career of the Harlem Renaissance poet and the generations that have followed. As one glances from Cullen to present works and back, it is sometimes hard to tell the difference. In short, Cullen offers a paradigm in the Black American creative experience, and summary appraisals of his work lead to obfuscation rather than the clarity we so sorely need. He wrote a number of outstanding romantic lyrics and contributed racial poems that will endure because they grant insight into the Black American dilemma. But perhaps it is fitting to allow his own guiding star to render the final judgment. John Keats defined our wisest stance toward Cullen when he wrote:

Men should bear with each other—there lives not the man who may not be cut up, aye hashed to pieces on his weakest side. . . . The sure way . . . is first to know a man's faults, and then be passive, if after that he insensibly draws you toward him then you have no power to break the link.[45]

Notes

1. Stephen H. Bronz, *Roots of Negro Racial Consciousness* (New York: Libra, 1964), pp. 64-65.
2. Countee Cullen, ed., *Caroling Dusk* (New York: Harper and Brothers, 1927), p. 179. All citations from *Caroling Dusk* in my text refer to this edition.
3. James Weldon Johnson, *Along This Way* (New York: Viking, 1968), p. 160.
4. Arna Bontemps, "The Negro Contribution to American Letters," in *The American Negro Reference Book* (Englewood Cliffs, New Jersey: Prentice-Hall, 1966), pp. 854-55.
5. W. E. B. Du Bois, "Criteria of Negro Art," *Crisis,* XXXII (1926), 296.
6. Darwin T. Turner, "Countee Cullen: The Lost Ariel," in *In a Minor Chord* (Carbondale: Southern Illinois University Press, 1971), pp. 60-88. Turner follows the lead of J. Saunders Redding, who called Cullen "the Ariel of Negro poets" in *To Make a Poet Black* (Chapel Hill: University of North Carolina Press, 1939), p. 111.
7. Nathan Irvin Huggins, *Harlem Renaissance* (New York: Oxford University Press, 1971), p. 206.
8. Fred Beauford, "A Conversation with Ishmael Reed," *Black Creation,* IV (1973), 13. The description is Reed's.
9. Blanche E. Ferguson, *Countee Cullen and the Negro Renaissance* (New York: Dodd, Mead, 1966), p. 41. This is currently the most complete published biography of Cullen, and I have relied heavily upon it for the information contained in my brief overview of the poet's life.
10. Arna Bontemps, "The Harlem Renaissance," *Saturday Review,* XXX (1947), 12.
11. Langston Hughes, *The Big Sea* (New York: Hill and Wang, 1963), pp. 311-330.
12. An interview with Marjorie Content Toomer conducted by Ann Allen Shockley for the Fisk University Black Oral History Program, Special Collections, Fisk University Library, Nashville, Tennessee.
13. In *Harlem Renaissance,* Nathan Huggins says: "It was Cullen who told Langston Hughes that he wanted to be a poet, not a Negro poet," p. 208. The author is referring to Hughes's introductory remarks in "The Negro Artist and the Racial Mountain." Hughes calls no names; Huggins lists one without a footnote.

14. W. E. B. Du Bois, "Our Book Shelf," *Crisis,* XXXI (1926), 239.
15. Alain Locke, "Negro Youth Speaks," in *The New Negro,* ed., Alain Locke (New York: Atheneum, 1968), p. 52.
16. James Weldon Johnson, ed., *The Book of American Negro Poetry* (New York: Harcourt, Brace & World, 1959), pp. 219-220.
17. Countee Cullen, "The Negro in Art," *Crisis,* XXXII (1926), 193.
18. Quoted from Darwin T. Turner, *op. cit.,* pp. 77-78.
19. Countee Cullen, "Countee Cullen on Miscegenation," *Crisis,* XXXVI (1929), 373.
20. Countee Cullen, "The Negro in Art," 194.
21. Countee Cullen, *Caroling Dusk,* p. xii.
22. Countee Cullen, "The Dark Tower," *Opportunity,* V (1927), 180.
23. Countee Cullen, *Caroling Dusk,* p. 180.
24. Quoted from Stephen Bronz, *op. cit.,* p. 58.
25. Quoted from Beulah Reimherr, "Race Consciousness in Countee Cullen's Poetry," *Susquehanna University Studies,* VII (1963), 67.
26. Countee Cullen, "The Negro in Art," 193.
27. Arna Bontemps, "The Harlem Renaissance," 44.
28. James Weldon Johnson, *The Book of American Negro Poetry,* p. 39.
29. Countee Cullen, *Caroling Dusk,* p. 179.
30. Countee Cullen, "To You Who Read My Book," in *Color* (New York: Harper and Brothers, 1925). All citations from *Color* in my text refer to this edition. In this and the following discussions, I have omitted line and page references: the reader can locate most of the quoted passages easily.
31. Bertram L. Woodruff, "The Poetic Philosophy of Countee Cullen," *Phylon,* I (1940), 213-223.
32. James Weldon Johnson, *The Book of American Negro Poetry,* p. 221.
33. Arthur P. Davis, "The Alien-and-Exile Theme in Countee Cullen's Racial Poems," *Phylon,* XIV (1953), 390.
34. The charges come from Stephen Bronz, *op. cit.,* and Darwin Turner, *op. cit.,* respectively.
35. In "Major Themes in the Poetry of Countee Cullen," in *The Harlem Renaissance Remembered,* ed., Arna Bontemps (New York: Dodd, Mead, 1972), pp. 115-118, Nicholas Canaday points out that both "Incident" and the later "Uncle Jim" are poems of initiation.
36. *Ibid.,* pp. 104-106. Canaday offers a good discussion of Cullen's pervasive use of religious imagery and forms.

37. James Weldon Johnson, *Along This Way*, p. 161.
38. Benjamin Brawley, *The Negro Genius* (New York: Dodd, Mead, 1937), p. 226.
39. Countee Cullen, *Copper Sun* (New York: Harper and Brothers, 1927). All citations from *Copper Sun* in my text refer to this edition.
40. W. K. Wimsatt, *The Verbal Icon: Studies in the Meaning of Poetry* (Lexington: University of Kentucky Press, 1954).
41. Harvey Curtis Webster, "A Difficult Career," *Poetry*, LXX (1947), 224.
42. "The Ballad of the Brown Girl, An Old Ballad Retold," in *On These I stand*, by Countee Cullen (New York: Harper and Row, 1947), pp. 175-182. All citations from *The Ballad of the Brown Girl* in my text refer to this version.
43. Countee Cullen, *The Black Christ and Other Poems* (New York: Harper and Brothers, 1929). All citations from *The Black Christ* in my text refer to this edition.
44. Countee Cullen, *The Medea and Some Poems* (New York: Harper and Brothers, 1935). All citations from *The Medea* in my text refer to this edition.
45. "John Keats to Benjamin Bailey, January 3, 1818," in *John Keats Selected Poems and Letters,* ed. Douglas Bush (Boston: Houghton Mifflin, 1959), p. 262.

Bibliography

Beauford, Fred. "A Conversation with Ishmael Reed." *Black Creation,* IV (1973), 12-15.

Bontemps, Arna. "The Harlem Renaissance." *Saturday Review,* XXX (1947), 12-13, 44.

——————. "The Negro Contribution to American Letters." In *The American Negro Reference Book.* Englewood Cliffs, N. J.: Prentice-Hall, 1966.

Brawley, Benjamin. *The Negro Genius.* New York: Dodd, Mead & Company, 1937.

Bronz, Stephen H. *Roots of Negro Racial Consciousness.* New York: Libra, 1964.

Bush, Douglas, ed. *John Keats Selected Poems and Letters.* Boston: Houghton Mifflin Company, 1959.

Canaday, Nicholas. "Major Themes in the Poetry of Countee Cullen." In *The Harlem Renaissance Remembered,* ed. Arna Bontemps, pp. 103-125. New York: Dodd, Mead & Company, 1972.

Cullen, Countee, ed. *Caroling Dusk.* New York: Harper and Bros., 1927.

——————. *Color.* New York: Harper and Brothers, 1925.

——————. *Copper Sun.* New York: Harper and Brothers, 1927.

——————. "Countee Cullen on Miscegenation." *Crisis,* XXXVI (1929), 373.

——————. *The Black Christ.* New York: Harper and Brothers, 1929.

——————. "The Dark Tower." *Opportunity,* V (1927), 180.

——————. *The Medea.* New York: Harper and Brothers, 1935.

——————. "The Negro in Art." *Crisis,* XXXII (1926), 193-194.

——————. *On These I Stand.* New York: Harper & Row, 1947.

Davis, Arthur P. "The Alien-and-Exile Theme in Countee Cullen's Racial Poems." *Phylon,* XIV (1953), 390-400.

Du Bois, W. E. B. "Criteria of Negro Art." *Crisis,* XXXII (1926), 290-297.

——————. "Our Book Shelf." *Crisis,* XXXI (1926), 239.

Ferguson, Blanche E. *Countee Cullen and the Negro Renaissance.* New York: Dodd, Mead & Company, 1966.

Huggins, Nathan Irvin. *Harlem Renaissance.* New York: Oxford University Press, 1971.

Hughes, Langston. *The Big Sea.* New York: Hill and Wang, 1963.

Johnson, James Weldon. *Along This Way.* New York: Viking Press, 1968.

————. ed. *The Book of American Negro Poetry.* New York: Harcourt, Brace & World, 1959.

Locke, Alain. "Negro Youth Speaks." In *The New Negro,* ed. Alain Locke, pp. 47-53. New York: Atheneum, 1968.

Reimherr, Beulah. "Race Consciousness in Countee Cullen's Poetry." *Susquehanna University Studies,* VII (1963), 65-82.

Turner, Darwin. *In a Minor Chord.* Carbondale: Southern Illinois University Press, 1971.

Webster, Harvey Curtis. "A Difficult Career." *Poetry,* LXX (1947), 222-225.

Wimsatt, W. K. *The Verbal Icon: Studies in the Meaning of Poetry.* Lexington: University of Kentucky Press, 1954.

Woodruff, Bertram L. "The Poetic Philosophy of Countee Cullen." *Phylon,* I (1940), 213-223.

If you like this book . . . A Many-Colored Coat of Dreams you will like some of our other books listed on the inside front cover or on our flyers. You can order them conveniently by mailing this order form.

enclose $_____ for the books listed below. (Add 25 cents for postage and handling.)

Author	Title	Price	No. of Copies	Total

Send me free subscription to Newsletter ☐

Send me free announcements of new books ☐

Postage and Handling _____.25

Grand Total $_____

Name_____

Address_____

City_____State_____Zip_____

Mail check or money order to

BROADSIDE PRESS

Dept. M.O., 12651 Old Mill Place   Detroit, Michigan 48238

DATE DUE

PRINTED IN U.S.A.